4-00

9/11 4x

CR✓

Hillclimbing

by Ed Youngblood

Consultant:
Hugh Fleming
Director, AMA Sports
American Motorcyclist Association

Capstone Books

an imprint of Capstone Press
Mankato, Minnesota

Capstone Books are published by Capstone Press
P.O. Box 669, 151 Good Counsel Drive, Mankato, Minnesota 56002
http://www.capstone-press.com

Library of Congress Cataloging-in-Publication Data
Youngblood, Ed.
   Hillclimbing/by Ed Youngblood.
   p. cm.—(Motorcycles)
   Includes bibliographical references and index.
   Summary: Examines the history of motorcycle hillclimbing and describes its
skills and equipment.
   ISBN 0-7368-0475-7
   1. Motorcycling—Juvenile literature. 2. Motorcycle racing—Juvenile literature.
[1. Motorcycling.] I. Title. II. Series.
GV1059.514.Y68 2000
796.7'5 —dc21   99-049328

Editorial Credits
Angela Kaelberer, editor; Timothy Halldin, cover designer and illustrator;
   Heidi Schoof and Jodi Theisen, photo researchers

Photo Credits
Archive Photos, 12
David Patton, cover, 4, 7, 8, 18, 21, 23, 24, 26, 29, 30, 32, 34, 37, 38, 41, 45
Tom Stimson/FPG International LLC, 10; FPG International LLC, 15

1 2 3 4 5 6 05 04 03 02 01 00

Table of Contents

Features

CHAPTER 1

Hillclimbing

Hillclimbing is a form of motorcycle competition. Hillclimbers race specially designed motorcycles to the tops of hills. The racer who reaches the top of the hill in the shortest amount of time wins.

Hillclimbing Motorcycles

Hillclimbers ride special, custom-built motorcycles. They are built one at a time with special features that allow them to climb hills more quickly. Hillclimbing motorcycles are about 3 feet (1 meter) longer than street motorcycles. Several manufacturers make engines used for hillclimbing motorcycles. These include Harley-Davidson, Kawasaki, and Honda.

Hillclimbers race motorcycles to the tops of hills.

Engine size is measured in cubic centimeters (ccs). Today, hillclimbers race either 540cc or 800cc motorcycles. Larger engines usually have more power. The 800cc motorcycles are faster and more powerful than the 540cc motorcycles.

Hillclimbing Organizations and Events
The American Motorcyclist Association (AMA) governs most hillclimbing events in North America. This group first organized motorcycle races in 1924. Today, the AMA sanctions most motorcycle races in North America. Sanctioned races are official AMA racing events. These events follow AMA rules and guidelines. The Canadian Motorcycle Association (CMA) sanctions events held in Canada.

The Professional Hill Climbers Association was formed in 1969. This organization works to promote hillclimbing.

Motorcycle organizations sanction both amateur and professional hillclimbing events. Amateur hillclimbers often have little or no

800cc motorcycles are faster and more powerful than 540cc motorcycles.

racing experience. They do not race for prize money. Professional hillclimbers have more experience. They can earn money for racing.

Most hillclimbers begin their racing career at an early age. The AMA sanctions events for hillclimbers younger than 16 years old. Young motorcyclists learn to race on small motorcycles. These motorcycles often are as

The Devil's Staircase is 500 feet (152 meters) high.

small as 50cc. At age 16, hillclimbers who do well in amateur races can obtain a professional license. This document allows hillclimbers to compete in AMA national championship events.

Professional hillclimbers compete in the AMA National Championship Series. This series includes 14 hillclimbing events. Hillclimbers can compete in either the 540cc class or the 800cc class. Less experienced hillclimbers usually compete in the 540cc class. These motorcycles are smaller and easier for less experienced hillclimbers to handle. They also are less expensive than 800cc motorcycles. Hillclimbers often move up to the 800cc class as they gain experience.

Hills

Most of the hills used for AMA national championship events are about 350 to 500 feet (100 to 150 meters) high. These hills are very steep. Some have steps or terraces carved into them. Hillclimbers must jump their motorcycles from step to step. This requires a great deal of skill. Only the most experienced hillclimbers attempt to climb hills with steps.

Some hills have interesting names. One is called the Widowmaker. This 650-foot (198-meter) hill is located near Salt Lake City, Utah. Another popular hill is the Devil's Staircase in Oregonia, Ohio. This hill is 500 feet (152 meters) high. Other well-known hills are located in Freemansburg and York, Pennsylvania.

CHAPTER 2

History

Hillclimbing is one of the oldest forms of motorcycle racing. It began in the early 1900s as a way to test motorcycles' reliability.

Early Motorcycles

In the late 1800s, European and North American inventors built the first motorcycles. They attached steam-powered engines to bicycles. These motorcycles were not very safe. Riders often sat directly above the engine. The engine's steam could burn the rider.

In 1876, German inventor Nikolaus Otto invented the internal combustion engine. This engine burns fuel inside the engine. In 1885, German engineer Gottlieb Daimler designed a

The sport of hillclimbing has changed little over the years.

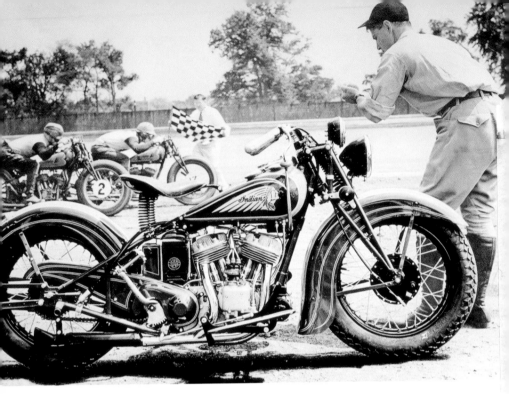

By 1900, many manufacturers were building motorcycles with internal combustion engines.

motorcycle with an internal combustion engine. This engine was safer and more efficient than steam-powered engines. By 1900, many companies in Europe and North America were building motorcycles with internal combustion engines.

Early motorcycle engines produced little power. They had only one cylinder. Fuel is burned in these spaces inside engines. The early engines produced only 1 or 2 horsepower. This unit measures an engine's power. Today's hillclimbing engines can produce as much as 200 horsepower.

The small engines usually worked well only on smooth, level ground. Engines also had a leather belt called a belt drive that turned the rear wheel. The belt drive often slipped when it became wet or muddy. The belt drive and the small engines made climbing hills a challenge. Manufacturers usually did not remove the bicycle pedals from the motorcycle. Riders could use the pedals if the small engine did not have enough power to climb hills.

Beginnings of Hillclimbing

Manufacturers began to test their motorcycles' reliability and strength by racing them up hills. By 1910, North American motorcycle clubs were organizing competitive hillclimbing events. Judges used a clock to determine which motorcyclist climbed the hill the fastest.

By the 1920s, motorcycle manufacturers were producing motorcycles with larger engines.

They removed the pedals and added a second cylinder. This allowed engines to produce more horsepower. Indian, Harley-Davidson, Cyclone, and Flying Merkel made some of the early two-cylinder motorcycles in North America. All of these companies became known for their ability to build powerful racing motorcycles. Harley-Davidson is the only one of these companies that still exists today.

By 1920, manufacturers had replaced the leather belt drive with a metal chain. The chain did not break or fall off as often as the leather belt did. This greatly improved motorcycles' reliability.

Changes in Hillclimbing

Improved motorcycles meant that hillclimbing events no longer just tested a motorcycle's strength and reliability. Most motorcycles were able to climb hills. A motorcycle's speed became more important to winning hillclimbing events.

Hillclimbing event organizers wanted to challenge hillclimbers. They organized events on steeper hills. Some were so steep that it was

Speed became an important part of winning hillclimbing events during the 1920s and 1930s.

nearly impossible for a person to stand on the side of the hill. Manufacturers and hillclimbers designed special motorcycles to quickly climb these steep hills.

In the 1920s, hillclimbing became even more popular in North America. One of the top hillclimbers during that time was Orie Steele of Ridgeway, New Jersey. In 1926, Steele competed in 49 events and set 22 hillclimbing records on his Indian motorcycle.

Hillclimbing's popularity decreased during the Great Depression (1929–1939). Few people had money to buy or race motorcycles during this time. The sport nearly disappeared during World War II (1939–1945). Gasoline was in short supply during the war. People needed gasoline for cars and military vehicles instead of motorcycle racing. Hillclimbing became popular again after the war ended.

Over the years, hillclimbing has included different classes. Hillclimbers would compete in either a larger or smaller engine class. In the late 1970s, hillclimbers competed in either the 500cc or 750cc class. Since 1988, hillclimbers have competed in the 540cc or 800cc classes.

History's Best Hillclimbers

Ten National Championships
Earl Bowlby; Logan, Ohio

Five National Championships
Joe Hemmis; Cumberland, Maryland
Paul Pinsonnault; Ludlow, Massachusetts
John Williams; Markham, Ontario

Four National Championships
Tim Frazier; Lancaster, Ohio
Terry Kinzer; Pikeville, Kentucky
Glen Kyle; Goshen, Indiana
Howard Mitzel; York, Pennsylvania
Greg Williams; Markham, Ontario

Three National Championships
Willard Bryan; Groveport, Ohio
Lou Gerencer, Jr.; Elkhart, Indiana
Lou Gerencer, Sr.; Elkhart, Indiana
James Large; Columbus, Ohio

CHAPTER 3

Equipment

Professional hillclimbers race modified motorcycles. These motorcycles are not street legal. They cannot be ridden on public streets or roads as street motorcycles can.

A Modified Machine

Hillclimbing motorcycles lack some of the safety equipment required for street motorcycles. Hillclimbing motorcycles do not have lights, mirrors, or turn signals. This equipment is not necessary for climbing hills. They also lack horns, speedometers, and mufflers. Mufflers reduce the noise produced by the motorcycle's engine. Hillclimbing motorcycles have only a small brake on the front wheel. They have no brake on the back

Hillclimbing motorcycles are not street legal.

wheel. Hillclimbing motorcycles also lack a front fender, windshield, or passenger seat.

Hillclimbing motorcycles weigh less than street motorcycles. This is because they lack so many parts. Professional hillclimbing motorcycles must be as lightweight as possible. Each hillclimbing motorcycle weighs about 350 pounds (160 kilograms). This is half the weight of many street motorcycles.

Wheelbase

Length is the most noticeable feature of a professional hillclimbing motorcycle. A hillclimbing motorcycle's wheelbase is about 8 feet (2.4 meters). The wheelbase is the distance between a motorcycle's front and rear axles. The wheels are attached to the axles. A street motorcycle has a wheelbase of about 5.5 feet (1.7 meters). A hillclimbing motorcycle's longer wheelbase helps prevent the motorcycle from flipping during uphill races.

The extra length is added to the back of the motorcycle with a long swingarm. All motorcycles have a swinging arm that allows

Length is a professional hillclimbing motorcycle's most noticeable feature.

the rear wheel to go over bumps more smoothly. Motorcyclists shorten "swinging arm" to "swingarm." The swingarm is attached to the motorcycle's frame by shock absorbers. These devices help the motorcycle's frame absorb bumps.

Most street motorcycles have rear wheels that move up and down 4 or 5 inches (10 to 13 centimeters). This allows these motorcycles to ride smoothly over street bumps. A hillclimbing motorcycle's rear wheel can move up and down 12 inches (30 centimeters) or more. This movement helps the motorcycle ride smoothly over a hill's rough land area. But this movement of the rear wheel also makes the motorcycle very tall. Hillclimbers sometimes have to stand on wooden blocks to hold their parked motorcycles upright.

Tires and Gears

Hillclimbing motorcycles use a modified rear tire. This tire easily races over loose dirt and rocks. The tire has better traction on these surfaces than a standard tire does.

Some hillclimbing motorcycles have a rear tire called a paddle tire. This tire has hard rubber scoops molded into its tread. These scoops help keep the tire from slipping on rough or muddy ground. Paddle tires look and work like paddle wheels on riverboats. They dig deep into the dirt and scoop it up in their treads. Other hillclimbers wrap chains around a standard tire to improve its traction.

Rear paddle tires look and work like paddle wheels on riverboats.

The Harley-Davidson XR-750 is one of the most popular hillclimbing motorcycle engines.

Hillclimbers also modify their motorcycles' transmissions. Street motorcycles have between four and six gears. Riders use lower gears to ride slowly through heavy traffic. They shift into higher gears to ride at higher speeds on freeways. Hillclimbing motorcycle transmissions include only the highest gear. This gear is all the motorcycles need to race quickly up hills. The motorcycle also weighs less with fewer gears.

Engines

Hillclimbing motorcycles use modified street motorcycle engines. The modified engines have more pressure in their cylinders. The amount of pressure is called compression. Engine power also is affected by how the valves open and close. The valves let fuel and air into the cylinder and let exhaust out. Devices called cams open the valves. Manufacturers change the shape of these cams. This changes the motion of the valves and makes the engine produce more power. These changes make the engines more than twice as powerful as street motorcycle engines.

The Harley-Davidson XR-750 is one of the most popular hillclimbing motorcycle engines. Harley-Davidson designed this engine for dirt track racing. The original engine produces about 100 horsepower. The same engine produces as much as 200 horsepower when modified for hillclimbing.

Hillclimbing Fuel

Most street motorcycles are equipped with a carburetor. This device mixes gasoline with oxygen before the gasoline is forced into the cylinders. The gasoline flows from the gas tank into the carburetor from the weight of gravity.

Hillclimbers modify their motorcycles to burn nitromethane instead of gasoline. Hillclimbers often call this powerful fuel "nitro." Some drag-racing cars and motorcycles also use nitromethane.

Nitro-burning motorcycles do not have carburetors. Instead, they have powerful pumps that feed fuel into injectors. Injectors are devices that quickly shoot fuel into the engine cylinders. Nitro-burning engines use fuel 10 times faster than gasoline-burning engines. A hillclimbing motorcycle can burn 1 gallon (3.8 liters) of nitro in less than 10 seconds.

Nitromethane is expensive. A hillclimber can burn $20 worth of fuel in a single run up a hill. Nitromethane is not available at gas stations. Hillclimbers must order it from

Hillclimbing motorcycles burn an explosive fuel called nitromethane.

companies that sell special racing fuels. Nitromethane also is a hazardous material. It explodes easily. This means it requires special handling. This adds to its cost.

Clothing and Helmets
Hillclimbers wear equipment and clothing that protect them from injuries. They wear boots, gloves, and full-coverage helmets. These helmets cover the hillclimber's entire face and head. Hillclimbers also wear leather or nylon riding suits. These suits help protect hillclimbers' skin during falls.

Most hillclimbers wear earplugs to protect their ears. Hillclimbing motorcycles create a great deal of noise. Nitromethane creates loud explosions in motorcycle engines. Hillclimbing motorcycles do not have mufflers to decrease this noise.

Hillclimbers wear full-coverage helmets and leather or nylon riding suits.

James Large

Born: December 23, 1968
Hometown: Columbus, Ohio
Turned Pro: 1995

AMA National Championships
1999
1998
1997

James Large is nicknamed "Jammer." He competes in the 800cc class on a modified Harley-Davidson XR-750 motorcycle. Large began hillclimbing in 1994 and turned professional in 1995. He became the AMA national champion in 1997, 1998, and 1999.

CHAPTER 4

Skills and Safety

Hillclimbing can be dangerous because of the steep hills and speeds involved. The American Motorcyclist Association develops rules for equipment, hillclimbers, and spectator behavior. Spectators are people who watch hillclimbing events. These rules help keep the sport safe.

Skills

Hillclimbers use both mental and physical skills to win competitions. Hillclimbing requires strength. But concentration, quick reflexes, and experience are more important.

Hillclimbers have only a few seconds to race to the top of a hill. They must concentrate and remain focused on the climb. They need good

---

Hillclimbers use both mental and physical skills to win competitions.

Hillclimbers begin each run in an area called the starting box.

reflexes. They must quickly react to obstacles on the course or to problems with their motorcycles. Hillclimbers practice these skills during each competition. Because of this, more experienced hillclimbers often have an advantage over less experienced hillclimbers.

Hillclimbing Events

One hillclimber climbs a hill at a time. Each hillclimbing attempt is called a run.

The hillclimbing course is marked with banners or ribbons. No one is allowed on the course while a racer is climbing the hill. An official stands at the top of the hill with a green flag. The official waves the green flag when the hill is safe to climb. Hillclimbers cannot begin racing until they receive this signal. Spectators are not allowed near the course or the starting zone. This helps protect spectators from injuries if a hillclimber loses control or crashes.

Hillclimbers begin each run in an area called the starting box. This area is located at the base of the hill. Hillclimbers back their motorcycles up to a log. They wait to receive a signal from a racing official. But they do not take off immediately. Hillclimbers usually open and close the motorcycle's throttle several times before taking off. The throttle is a valve that controls the engine's speed. It opens and closes to let fuel and air into the engine.

Hillclimbers open the throttle to give the engine more fuel. This gives the engine more power. They close the throttle to decrease the engine's power. They do this to make sure the engine is running smoothly. The hillclimber then opens the throttle all the way and releases the clutch. This makes the motorcycle move forward.

The motorcycle sets off a photocell when it leaves the starting box. This electronic device starts a clock. The motorcycle sets off another photocell at the top of the hill. This photocell stops the clock. Officials time the climbs to one-thousandth of a second. Top hillclimbers can climb a 500-foot (152-meter) hill in about eight seconds. They can climb a 400-foot (122-meter) hill in about six seconds.

At most events, hillclimbers get two runs up the hill. At some events, they get three runs. The hillclimber with the fastest climb of the day wins the competition.

Safety Equipment

Hillclimbing motorcycles have some safety equipment. This equipment protects both hillclimbers and spectators from injuries.

Each hillclimbing motorcycle has a kill switch on the handlebars. This device breaks the electrical circuit that supplies power to the

The motorcycle's large rear fender protects hillclimbers from the spray of dirt and rocks.

engine. A cord connects the kill switch to the hillclimber's arm. The engine immediately stops if the hillclimber falls or crashes.

The motorcycle must have a self-closing throttle. This throttle has springs that automatically close the throttle if hillclimbers release their grip. The motorcycle also has a large rear fender. This protects the hillclimber

Earl Bowlby's hillclimbing career lasted nearly 40 years.

from the spray of dirt and rocks during a climb. It also keeps the hillclimber from falling into the chain or the paddle tire during a crash.

Top Hillclimbers
Many hillclimbers have long careers. One such hillclimber is Earl Bowlby of Logan, Ohio. Bowlby began racing during the 1950s. He competed in more than 125 professional

hillclimbs during his career. He finished first or second in more than half of them. Bowlby earned 10 AMA national championship titles. He won his last national championship in 1990. In 1991, he retired at the age of 57.

Many families are involved in hillclimbing. Hillclimbers' families often travel with them to events. They may work as crew members or mechanics. This sometimes encourages family members to begin hillclimbing themselves.

One such family is the Gerencer family of Elkhart, Indiana. Lou Gerencer is a Harley-Davidson dealer. He sponsored his own hillclimbing team for many years. He was the AMA 750cc national champion in 1980, 1982, and 1987. His son Lou Gerencer, Jr. was a member of his crew. Today, Lou Gerencer, Sr. is retired and works on his son's crew. Lou Gerencer, Jr. won the AMA 800cc national championship in 1991, 1994, and 1996.

John Williams and his son Greg are from Markham, Ontario. They hold nine championship titles between them. John Williams won his titles in 1972, 1977, 1979,

1980, and 1981. Greg Williams won the 500cc championship in 1985, 1986, and 1987. He was the 540cc champion in 1989.

Cathy Templeton of Manchester, Connecticut, is the first female professional hillclimber. Templeton followed her brothers Robert and Michael into hillclimbing. In 1996, Templeton became the first woman to earn an AMA amateur hillclimbing national championship. In 1997, she became the first woman to receive an AMA professional hillclimbing license. She was 17 years old at the time. The AMA does not have separate classes for men and women. Templeton competed in the 540cc class against male hillclimbers.

The top hillclimbers earn prize money for competing. But most hillclimbers compete because they enjoy the sport's physical and mental challenges. Hillclimbers work to keep the sport safe and popular for future generations of hillclimbers and fans.

Cathy Templeton is the first female professional hillclimber.

Words to Know

axle (AK-suhl)—a rod that connects to the center of a wheel and holds the wheel in place

carburetor (KAR-buh-ray-tur)—a part of the engine that mixes oxygen with fuel before it is forced into the engine cylinders

clutch (KLUHCH)—a lever that allows a motorcycle rider to shift gears

cubic centimeter (KYOO-bik SENT-uh-mee-tur)—a unit that measures the size of a motorcycle's engine; this unit is abbreviated "cc."

cylinder (SIL-uhn-dur)—the space inside an engine where gasoline is burned

horsepower (HORSS-pou-ur)—a unit that measures an engine's power

internal combustion engine (in-TUR-nuhl kuhm-BUSS-chuhn EN-juhn)—an engine that burns fuel inside the engine

nitromethane (nye-troh-MEH-thane)—a highly explosive fuel used in hillclimbing motorcycle engines

photocell (FOH-toh-sel)—an electronic device that senses light

spectator (SPEK-tay-tur)—a person who watches an event

throttle (THROT-uhl)—a device that controls a vehicle's speed; a motorcycle throttle works like a car's gas pedal.

wheelbase (WEEL-bayss)—the distance between a motorcycle's front and rear axles

To Learn More

Dregni, Michael. *Motorcycle Racing.*
MotorSports. Mankato, Minn.: Capstone
Books, 1994.

Jay, Jackson. *Motorcycles.* Rollin'. Mankato,
Minn.: Capstone Books, 1996.

Otfinoski, Steven. *Wild on Wheels:
Motorcycles Then and Now.* Here We Go!
New York: Marshall Cavendish, 1998.

Savage, Jeff. *Motorcycles.* Race Car Legends.
Philadelphia: Chelsea House Publishers,
1997.

Useful Addresses

American Motorcyclist Association
13515 Yarmouth Drive
Pickerington, OH 43147

Canadian Motorcycle Association
P.O. Box 448
Hamilton, ON L8L 1J4
Canada

Professional Hill Climbers Association
1533 Hunsecker Road
Bird-in-Hand, PA 17505

Internet Sites

American Motorcyclist Association
http://www.ama-cycle.org

Canadian Motorcycle Association
http://www.canmocycle.ca

Cycle News
http://www.cyclenews.com

Index